For Tony

"He was the conch shell and the purple-fish left
by the lake tides."
—H.D.
Notes on Thought and Vision

Contents

One: The Needle's Eye

Learning How to Pray

When I die, I will practice the humble submission
of folded hands and lowered head,
swarming forward in that endless line of familiars,
inching on my knees toward the gates.

No doubt I will be sent away to school,
a beginning course in patience or compassion,
a lower level internship that won't lead
to feathery wings or a gold nimbus.

I wonder if I will be held to the bodhisattva vow
I made only half awake—promising
to come back to this sad planet, again and again,
until the last sentient being is free?

I will wish I had prayed more, not those long winded
babblings and desperate pleas for things
I thought I needed, but small prayers,
their crumpled faces teary eyed, bleating thank you.

I will unravel the bone mala and wooden rosary
to pray the old beads of adoration,
roll the smooth round words of love
over and over between my fingers and thumb.

Maybe as I float up out of this body it will become clear
—the name of that guardian angel at my shoulder,
the smell of earth like frankincense and myrrh,
all creatures tumbling under the canopy of clouds.

The Gift of Tongues

Once, we knew words were magic.
The round mouth of the moon opened and shut.
Fires of dung and brushwood made rings of light.
All things spoke the same language.

Before we speak, we must borrow some air.
A deep breath takes in millions of molecules once
breathed by Sappho. In this great cloud
old wisdom waits, drifting among the rubble.

That ecstasy of the gods is coming toward us.
The vocal cords begin to stretch and twang.
The flap of flesh hung from the soft
palate starts to shake. And the tongue trembles.

When the rush of a mighty wind draws near—
tongues of fire will appear, part, come to rest
on each startled body. We open our mouths amazed
as gilded moths fly into this new night.

We practice the seven vowel sounds and the sacred
tones, hum the seed syllables tied to the body,
recite the unspoken name of God. The wind fills
with a perfect pandemonium of words.

Ichthyology

Rib of carp, I will tell your strange story.
At the Buddhist temple by a river in Burma
I bought flowers, and popcorn sewn on a string,
then knelt down and fed the whiskered butterfish
that thrashed and spun in the brown water.

Fish hold the history of the world inside the shapes
of their bones. I am floating down a river
curled inside bones bent like staves of a boat,
twisted tooth of moon, an unstrung bow, a fish bone
caught in the throat.

Fish paint the story of the world in the colors
of their scales, every stipple dot fleck speckle
an iridescent sequin. I did not know scales are bone,
formed in the membrane of skin.

In the rays of fins the world rises, fanned out,
a spoked sun of cartilage. Watery wings open
and close. They are a spread web, gauzy fabric of gills
to breathe water by.

Early Christians claimed themselves alongside roads
by drawing fish in the chalky white dust.
With the tip of a rod or a staff, they drew the snout
and humble body.

A fish laid out on a wooden table stares
with bruised eye, lips flattened and rolled back.
This is the mystery silently spoken
long before the dreary portraits of bread and wine.

Basho's Frog

A frog went plop in a pond three hundred years
ago and still the sound is clear as the shimmer
and thrum of a struck gong.

Blood flows through the three chambered heart
and frogs close their eyes much as humans do,
a thin piece of flesh sewn to the bottom lid.

When I was a child, two brothers took me deep
into the forest. They caught bright green frogs
and strung them on long stems.

The webbed feet peddled slowly through space,
eyes bulged in the short neckless bodies,
smooth lips mouthed O.

Once I saw a young frog pull its tight skin
over its head like a sweater. It shed
the membrane too delicate to filter foul things

from the air. The dwindling numbers
and oddly made limbs fill me with sorrow,
the polliwogs with their missing eyebuds.

I would kneel on the damp cellar floor to hear
again the bullfrog who came each winter
into the drain, his grunt and throaty murmur.

If I squint, I can almost make out a frog
on the moon (totem of witches and crones).
It sits squat on that luminous leafpad.

In Praise of Feet

Some can walk over burning coals.
They know things the head has forgotten:
how the earth presses toward us,
calling out beneath concrete or bent grass.

Their soles hold messages, findings from a long
journey downward. Layers of callus rise,
or the bubble of a blister with its dainty skin.

The feet of Chinese women were once bound
(broken bones folded in the too large skin)
the stumps fitted with lotus shoes
three inches long.

They are not the flat muscular feet of snails.
They are not talons, pads, or paws,
this woven maze of vessel and nerve.

Seventy two thousand nerve endings meet
at the bottoms of the feet, the ears—
a point beneath the little toe, the appendix—
a vestigial pouch under the right heel.

Some feet dance in vats of red or purple grapes,
turn berries to wine. Later they uncurl,
then stretch. When in ecstasy, the toes arch
instinctively upward.

Inflammation

*The Roman physician Celsus in the first century C.E. identified
the four cardinal signs of inflammation.*

Rubor
Even if hidden to the naked eye, it persists
around the edges, the first faint tint of pink,
then red. The agent of grace arrives, taking its place
among the lines of an unsuspecting life. It is an intruder,
this sliver of spirit—colored portwine, or vermilion.

Calor
Soon the heat deepens. The heart turns to fire:
blood looping through the body like molten rock.
The heat creeps into fingerbone and voicebox.
We are seared and scalded, fevered by the breaking in
of an unknown guest.

Tumor
The red fire wells and billows. It is a knurl,
a knob, a holy node. It fattens and bloats, welling up
into any space that offers itself—a borrowed ear,
a cupped hand, the blank page. It bulges,
outspread, grafted from a source beyond measure,
and known only as: not this, not that.

Dolor
We ache from kindled passion. Ache turns to wrack
of woe, then wreath of thorns. Pierced
and wholly stung, pain rises from the body's own
withering reply. Offer up a tangle of weeping sheets.
Become locus of new life, host to the lowly, livid
with all manner of shadowform—and on fire.

Enoch Tells the Secrets of the Sixth Day

The fifth day of course was busy, the sea
bringing forth the fishes, monkfish and angelfish,
the skates and rays, and squid spurting their dark ink,
and then the feathered things filling the air—

screech owls and oystercatchers, the sky
peppered with ravens and crows. Locusts murmured
about the nine plagues, forming swarms. Gadflies flitted
and woodworms fretted their trails.

The crawling things appeared on the earth and roamed,
nudging the grasses with snuffling noses.
They made their way across prairies of gilded wheat,
and sifted through the sands with cloven or unsplit feet.

Male and female creatures coupled. The noise
was immense: moos and squeals, honking and trumpeting,
the caterwauls of beasts in heat. Nighttime fell and stars
rowed out in their boats across the purpled firmament.

When the sixth day dawned, the time came
to form man from the wisdom of God. The formula
for the seven components was simple. Flesh was made
from the earth, clammy gray clay, sod, bole and loam.

Blood was wrung from the dewdrops which hung
in spheres on leafblades and flower lips,
and eyes were plucked from the sun and pushed
into the sockets like fallen embers.

Bones were built of stone—marble, flint and slate,
and the long bones stuffed with marrow.
Man's intellect was taken from the swiftness of angels
and gauzy clouds skimming the earth.

Veins and hair were formed from the thin bodied grasses,
hollowed out and strung together. The soul
was made of God's breath blown down a strawblade
along the lean body of the wind.

After this came the story of the rib, about which
I longed to warn the Creator, saying:
make the woman first, let her prevent what will become
a miserable dominion over the earth.

Redemption

All the world is lit with God's light.
It lingers within the lowly places, in the deep
underbelly of things—

In bars where the zealous keep a kind of
communion, their glasses raised.

On misshapen faces, bruised by fists
that leave flowers of flesh (purple, then green)
before fading into memory of muscle and cell.

On the clear drop that trembles at a needle's tip.
In a spent droplet at the head of a shaft.

In poison rain falling on untilled fields.
In the drip and mire of sewage seeping.

In the palsied walk of withered women
making their way over bridges and up alleyways
in Los Angeles and Paris, anywhere at all.

It glimmers in the eye of the atom where charged
particles hurl. And the white cloud of light
bellows the one unknown word.

The Black Arts

I adore the pitch black nature of life,
the sloe swarthiness of raven and crow

how black sheep wander the pastures of desire
to find their way moonless back home

how it is the shadow that makes us human,
the dark image we cast, sepulcher of gold

how from a black hole light cannot leave
yet like worm holes through soil
these tunnels join universe to universe

how during the night we pull up covers
and turn down layers of sleep to the dreamworld
where we tell our selves stories

how alchemists call part of the journey to self
negredo melancholia, a black that is even
blacker than black

how out of the earth comes volcanic obsidian,
its glossy curves, and when the fringed lips
of the oyster are parted—perhaps a black pearl

how the black Madonna holds in her arms a tiny
black Christ, the two dressed in robes and crowns

how still the waters are in the dark wine
of the womb.

The Naming of Things

We name the world to console ourselves.
Hands point to the numbers on a clock.
Sipping tea from a cup, we place lip upon lip
and drink rose hips, fleshy center of the flower.

The bulbous legs of a table remind me of a relative
from the old country. They sink down
into the flowery crimson carpet, unbudging
and thick with dignity.

The metal teeth of a saw bite into limbs
to spit out chips of pine and oak.
The teeth of a comb can find white lice that love
the delicate hairs at the nape of a neck.

Through the mouth of a cave, through limestone
built of tiny sea bodies, we enter the earth.
Veins of ore run through rock, variegated
layers of lodestone and gold.

In the puckered navel of an orange the unborn fruit
is tucked. A beetle crawls along the leathery neck
of a squash. Eyes look back at us from the leaf bud
of a potato, from the still center of a cyclone—

no rain in sight. We walk on bound soles
in transitory bodies. Spines of leatherbound books
list the ways of longing, spell out our loneliness
in the nominal world.

Practicing for the Rapture

Instantly they grew wings: the rocks that soared.
—Pablo Neruda

In the grainy frames of an early film, a man straps on
a contraption of wings and runs downhill, his arms
flapping wildly.

Below him the sleeves of shirts pegged to a clothesline
snap in the wind, longing to loosen
and sail.

In the park, men on benches hold open their newspapers,
the black words basking in sunlight,
unfolding their serifs.

The wind lifts a nun's wimple as she crosses the street.
Only the solid body and heavy shoes
weigh her down.

In the community pool, swimmers do the butterfly stroke,
muscled arms drawn upward out
of the undulant water.

The nocturnal moth resting in the rafters is bemused,
its paired wings outspread
and dotted with dust.

Outside of town, drawbridges raise their steel struts above
the busy river. Along the breakwater,
the riprap shudders

thinking of growing wings. The wet boulders make ready
to rise, and enter a realm of creatures
lighter than air.

Supplication

She places an orange leaf in every fingerbowl.
There are seven of them lined up in a row,
hammered from brass and glimmering in the light.

She pours water from a pitcher, splashing her hands
and then filling each bowl.

She recites an odd liturgy: a jumble of Latin
and Sanskrit, palatal clicks, a flicking of the tongue.

Before the altar she kneels, backbone straight
as a candlestick, heart the tallow and wick.

She prays for all places in the world where the bodies
of children lie safe, at last, in the forgiving earth.

It is earth that lifts from stiffened flesh, mends
defilement and wound. She praises the wingtip
and touch of each angel.

In the darkness, thin robe wrapped around her,
she pulls handfuls of gray eucalyptus leaves
from the tree beyond her yard.

The leaves are round and webbed with veins.
She presses them in saffron, deep orange, aromatic,
dried stigmata of crocus flowers crushed.

The mornings rise, orange leaves like small suns
floating in every bowl.

The Pharisees Are Scolded for Reading Scripture Literally

You blind guides, straining out a gnat and swallowing a camel!
—Matthew 23:24

It fell into my tea, its black thumbs thrashing,
eyes peering at the leaves sunk deep in the cup.
Swimming around the rim, the white hole of my abyss,
a troublesome midge.

I picked up a spoon and ladled it out of the drink.
Its two wings were twirling wildly. Already the swarm
was moving away, a dark cloud looking for others
reading that good book word for word.

I prayed the gnat wouldn't give me pinkeye
or the tropical yaws. I watched the dot of its body
laid down on a white napkin. I counted every hair
on its nose.

Meanwhile the camel folded himself into a tight ball.
Fresh from slipping through the eye
of a needle, he was humming sweetly
through his thick lips.

First one hoof slipped into the brew,
then the body, and at last the blubbery hump.
I did not notice him floating, I did not see.
He sank, gurgling, a sound like: hucka hucka hucka.

But the dregs of my tea tasted strongly of dates.
And at the bottom of my cup
I found a long dark eyelash, curled up
like a little noose.

Two: Tumbling in the Bower

Instructions for Walking on Water

When setting foot onto the water, keep in mind
the insubstantial line between above and below.

The thrill of stepping on a flimsy surface, reflection
glittering like beaten gold, can cause you to sink.

Schools of silvery fish swim up to see the source
of this outlandish shadow and find no boat.

Water striders skim across, whirligig beetles reel,
and soon your own feet scarcely ripple the surface.

You love Buddha telling of those *who without sinking
walk on water as if on earth*, and the Sea of Galilee.

When the dazed and weary eye of the sun blinks shut,
the moon lays down its mantle glinting like a mirror.

There are twice as many stars, two startled moons,
and you no longer care which way leads up or down.

Absolution

Travel to the great church at Cluny, and Pope Innocent
the Second would grant an indulgence. I drop to my knees
with Benedictines in the abbey, clear stony fields

and tend their gardens of root vegetables and grapes.
By giving a small sum for the chapel's adornment,
the belfry tower built of gray stone, a sinner pays for his sins.

I look for ways to absolve what sin lingers in this life.
In San Francisco I fasted for a week, only water
and sips of grape juice. My body began to levitate.

I drifted down Market Street, rode the rapid transit
through tunnels to Berkeley, floated past Telegraph Avenue
buoyant as a red balloon.

Years later in the heat of day, I wrote my greatest fear
on a slip of paper and walked over burning coals to the wet
pavement beyond. True believers leaped before me.

One kicked the embers, danced in a flowering of sparks.
I paused partway and blisters soon blossomed
on the bottoms of my feet.

At long last I limped into a church. Accepting the sacrament
of penance, I condensed the sins of forty years
into thirty minutes.

Kneeling before the black curtain I recited: *Bless me father,*
for I have sinned,
this is my first confession.

I offered to give details of long nights grasping for a vision
of God, the foul words that flew,
how little I loved myself, and why.

The priest had no need for more stories and the tedious
articles of despair. He said:
Go, and sin no more.

Others have looked for sacred relics: the finger or tooth
of a saint, a lock of hair. A fragment of shroud. Wood, bone,
ivory, quartz, a tiny Tibetan stupa built of bronze.

Maybe I could learn to make ritual instruments
from the bones of holy persons—begin to play that flute
or drum, contemplate a scoop made out of a skull cap.

I want to join the communion of saints, enter the mystical
body, paint on my door the words on the Imperial Cathedral
in Speyer, 1451: *In this place is full pardon of all sins.*

Noah's Ark

It was one of my oldest toys, the ark my father made
for me. He carved the base from a solid block,
lumber he called gopher wood, sealed the seams with pitch.

It had eight polished figures—hippos, camels, kangaroos,
necks bent, ready to stoop below the deck,
long bearded Noah and his nameless wife.

Old Noah, ninth in descent from Adam, the man/woman
God split in two. Nine generations and already
the world was corrupt, in need of annihilation.

One hundred and fifty days on that great flooded sea,
raven flew in search of land. Then dove, who found raven
asleep in an olive tree.

Mount Ararat is sacred to Armenians, the first race
to appear after the deluge. On Ararat grow juniper trees,
a few birch groves, the parched pasture grass.

Sheep graze, snow wraps the land, and water is scarce.
Where did the waters go that once covered the high hills
under the whole heavens?

My father, the carpenter, is dying. He can no longer build
wooden turtles sturdy enough to ride on,
a jigsaw puzzle of animal pieces.

His legs are splotched with time, skin raised in papery
layers. He sits in his chair, hands shuddering like wings,
like birds eager to lift.

Eve Wakes in the Garden

On the first day she wakes under a shade
of flowers, wondering who she is, and where?
The air is a warm breath.

She follows the sound of trickling, lies down
on the mossy bank of a brook
and looks into the clear blue mirror.

A face stares back at her: eyes drawn
like almonds, lips full as leaves. A voice says
she is looking at her own reflection

and there is someone like her, waiting, impatient.
She is led along a leaf-strewn path to Adam.
O, she thinks when she sees him—

he is not nearly as soft or pleasing as my image.
She turns back, but Adam pleads
for her to stay. He calls her: his flesh,

the very bone, she who was brought into being
from his side, nearest his heart.
She feels giddy, a sensation like whirling.

She has not yet plucked that red fruit
ripe as her own breast, or bit into soft flesh.
He kneels down to name the hunger in his thighs

and soon they are tumbling in the bower
on a bed of pink lobelia. Where is that snake
slung from the tree of knowing, slack body

ready to stiffen, its muscled length dangling
as though created for her pleasure? The day
is hot, the smell of blossoms thick about her.

I Want to Live as a Magician

It is not easy to move about on this earth with crumpled
wings, a fractured heart, my little
bundle of tricks.

I wake to sunlight flickering through palm fronds.
Some days the heckling sun has questions, the light
confused if it is particle or wave.

I sit with crossed legs on a cushion made of kapok.
My mind can see the cottony blossoms
strung at the ends of branches.

How many trees fall in the rainforest between two
breaths? How do the silky fibers smell,
burning to ash in the balmy air?

I keep a collection of photographs in rosewood frames:
Rimbaud dressed like a seer,
the Blessed Virgin crying blood red tears,

a Chinese soldier with his machine gun.
He stood at Khodari, closing down the border to Tibet.
I traveled there by truck from Katmandu.

Each deep bow of my body that day was for the Buddha
and the soldier. Sliding onto frozen soil, touching
my forehead to the ground,

my thirty three grand prostrations made him angry,
and the sandalwood mala, wrapped
like a rosary around my wrist.

If Whitman says our very being can become a poem,
then anything is possible. The same energy
that spins in reactors burns a gaunt body onto the shroud.

I will plant ten thousand trees, make real rabbits
out of my fingers and thumb, pull a host of doves
from my pocket and perch them on blooming branches.

Finding the Buddha

In the corner of a garden shop, among the evergreens
and azaleas, you sat alone on a table.
I carried you home to the shelf above my bed.

You sit serenely in lotus pose. Your hands gesture
meditation, palms like open bowls.
They rest on the soles of your upturned feet.

I light sticks of incense, jasmine and saffron, lavender
and rose, watch the stems of smoke
curl and wither.

I know somewhere in the cast blackness
of your form—you are alive. I feel you watching me,
how the dark garden of my life wilts and then

as if by a miracle, grows back once again,
and how the lovers come and go, one after another,
like blossoms falling.

I run my thumb over eyelids smooth as petals,
along the ripe lips, down the long leafstalk
of your earlobes. You are seed and root.

The flower of your mouth unfolds, bees bumping
against the body, your smile nearly ready
to bloom.

Tantric Sex

You hold a chrysanthemum blossom for me
(the dark orange flower, nearly red)
and cupped in your hands it becomes a mandala

—its rounded head a design of sensual petals
and a deep center where I, sick with longing,
might enter.

Your lips are smooth. I want to ride the warm breath
of a chant, suck the sweet ends of your thumbs.
Soon, you say. We drink white wine.

Legs in lotus pose, you look to me like a demigod—
a fair skinned fakir with brown hair, cheek slit
by a scar above the left tip of your mouth.

I slide onto the shaft, the hard lingam now holy.
The breath wants to catch in this throat
that can only hum.

The bones of my pelvis are a handle, a haft,
the hilt by which you lift me. We sway back and forth,
all night the candles burning.

The Buddha's Final Night

After eating the spoilt pork and consoling the man
who brought the poor pig, he lay down to die.
Or it may have been truffles or mushrooms that he ate,
the word *pig's soft food* no longer translatable.

He must have been weary of preaching the dharma
to whores, kings, and thieves. How often would he hear
the grumblings from monks upset at women among them?
Perhaps next time he would keep quiet about the miracle
under the fig tree, or teach only the ruminant deer.

The ground beneath the mango trees was soft.
Small pink flowers shook loose from their clusters
and fell upon his curled topknot, the long lobes of his ears.
The pain pricked his stomach like bamboo sticks.

He crossed the river to a grove of sala trees, laid
in lion's pose, broad head pressed to his right hand.
If he looked away from the weeping faces, up through
leaves of the trees, he could see a sky blue as turquoise.
Day wobbled on its wheel toward night.

The black opening of his eyes would soon widen.
He told his followers to become their own lamps.
He blew out the flame of this life and burned
into the heavens. Earth shuddered and the night sky
filled with the mournful face of the moon.

Rilke's Angels

At times it must be sad to be one of them,
hovering alone and unseen. They whirl
in their odd orbits, coiled springs of luminosity,
and very seldom smile.

They have names we do not know.
In fields and rooms they spin like children,
innocent, enraptured by the blurring
of their own bodies.

They take care not to muddle or mislay
their singular blessings and prayers.
It is a covenant they have entered into,
this constant turning and litany.

They might take pride in their work,
if such a sin were permitted. Instead
they are content with rumors, the occasional
resplendent vision.

When they reel and brush by, the air thickens
and turns to rosewood and myrrh.
They are felt as the shudder of a beating wing,
a terribly astonished breath.

The Dream of the Rood
after the 10th century C.E. Vercelli Book

Standing at the edge of the grove,
among blue ash and black oak,
I saw the men coming
and wanted to take up my roots.
The ax whittled bark and flesh
and I fell toward them. The work was hard,
the criminals a paltry lot, sweating and groaning
all the way up the hill,
and after uttering their death cry,
the lowly rattle of their bone box.
When the One Man laid his arm
along my crossbar, when he embraced me
like a bridegroom, I dared not droop
or bend. The spiked nails burrowed
through us and we did not fall.
It is true the earth trembled.
My sap turned red as blood. It seeped
through the holes of spear shafts
and knots where stems once grew.
Night came, and the cloud gloom thickened.
They took us down and put us
apart in the earth. For Him
the stone rolled away and He rose up, new.
I waited among worms and rootstalk.
After four hundred years St. Helena found me
in the dark earth. Pulled up into day,
gold and silver were hung
from my trunk, gemstones set about me.
Angels spun till they were blurs of light,
their wings droning. There I swayed
between gilded and bloodied
between glory and sorrow. I do not mind

the parings and carvings, relics
enough to fill a ship's hold,
for my form will never lessen.
I do not need a dreamer to speak for me.
Put your ear to the trunk of any tree, and listen.

The Annunciation

Federico Fiori (Barocci), oil on canvas, 1528

She is reading, her brown hair pulled back
from the unblemished forehead. The fluttering
in the nearby air and a flowery scent have startled her.
She drops the small book of psalms, and the blue mantle
(loose about her shoulders) falls to the footstool.

The angel kneeling before her has a celestial
aura, as though his luminous form
were carved of alabaster or made from white pearls.
He is holding a stem of lilies in his left hand
and with his right he reaches toward her, open palm

swollen, fingers unmistakably pointing to her.
The wings are a shimmer of blue, heavenly as sky.
He is saying something of great urgency,
how she has found favor with God, that soon
she will give birth to a son.

She is young and his words confuse her.
How can she be made with child when she does not
know a man? And yet, she thinks, he is such a glorious
angel, the golden curls spilling down his neck,
the firm rise of his wings.

She does not think of herself as a slave. The oil spills
willingly. The holy spirit, like the shadow
of some wild dark dove, falls upon her. The child leaps
within her belly. Already her heart is blossoming,
spreading its tender red stain.

Translation of the Holy House
altarpiece of the Madruzzo chapel in S. Onofrio, Rome

The house is brown, a simple framed structure
with a portico around the humble doors. And I can see
there are square darkened windows upstairs.

Mary looks glorious seated on the rooftop
in a blue satin gown, a puffy cloud unfolding
beneath her bare toes.

The child in her lap is happily pouring water
from a gilded jar onto the damned who rise
small and miserable among the flames of purgatory.

But it is the five angels who draw my eye,
the two holding the crown above Mary's head,
three transporting the house. The angel in the middle

has a muscled back bent to the task, arms
spread wide, feathered wings trembling, and the mauve
tip of his penis is visible between massive thighs.

Mary flies through seventeenth century
Italian skies, on the way to her role as mediatrix
for souls in limbo, for sailors drowning at sea.

She has that flushed windburned look of the chosen,
the slightly crimson cheeks of someone
traveling over a great distance at a spirited pace.

Sacrilegious

Above the white linen altar cloth the figure of Jesus
slumps on the cross. He wears a blackberry thorn wreath,
the purple berries dark as dried blood, his skin
gleaming along the cleavage of ribs.

If only I could climb up high and tie on a plush robe,
daub a little lip balm on those parched lips,
help staunch the flow from the hole in his side.
I am feeling a little sick.

We say we are unworthy to gather up the crumbs
from under that table. I think how hungry he must be
(the old thoughts meandering forsaken through his skull)
as he hangs there mostly naked on that cross.

I cannot speak of this. At times I see whirling,
there in the air, a spectral light, face like a fiery sun.
Have you seen it? I smile up through green leaves
haloed in gold and filled with leafblood.

I come from a family of mystics and seers. I come from
a long line of Anglican clergy. My great grandmother
was a Jew and no one told us. I am sorry, Ida Greenaway,
for the years you spent locked inside my father's mind.

It was prophesied that in the end times, the lost tribes
of Israel would amend and reform.
Who will dare to speak the sacred names of God?
Who will say Hashem, or Yeshua?

My son knows he is chosen. He finds it ironic
the Mayan calendar ends the day he turns twenty-eight:
December 23rd in the year of our lord 2012.
He is already packing his bags for the new world.

Who will write the history of our peoples?
Who will triangulate the stars this time, to settle
on a mountain top, squat in a forest beside the bromeliads
climbing the sacrificial trees?

Who will build pyramids to house the secrets of fusion
and levitation, summon up how to move heavy stones
(huge lips pouting out over the seas)
lifted up out of nothing?

Algorithms and the infinitude of pi—sixteenth letter
of the Greek alphabet, mystery of the circle.
Bring on the transcendental numbers and imaginary
numbers too, the square root of negative one.

Once I tried to explain Archimedes' quadrature of the circle
on a black board with yellow chalk
my voice breaking, the space between my thighs
quivering from the beauty of that theorem

which Miss X said was *no proof*, which I had *all wrong*,
and so I went to sleep in math and did not wake up,
unlearned the elegant language of the universe,
one into two and then the triangles transposing their domes.

My first universe was the cosmos of South D Street,
green house on the corner and around back, the cement steps
that led past the laurel hedge down the stairwell,
branches sinking into roots to enter the cellar.

Go away from the door to my scriptorium. I am sharpening
my quills, mixing the black ink, violet blue as plum juice.
I breathe in the holy breath, say my oblations, take
the sacred things to honor them on the altar of the earth.

I will pull on the green wool sweater and go for a walk
in the woods, kneel down to the flowering dogwood,
flog my shoulder with a weeping willow, lay a moth wing
on my tongue and let it melt there like the Host.

Three: Reading the Clues

Silent Reading

Saint Augustine was baffled when he found
the bishop Ambrose of Milan bent over a page
and soundlessly reading.
"Voice and tongue were silent," he writes awestruck
in the fourth century *Confessions.*

This was thought the oldest account of reading
noiselessly, not moving the lips.
Augustine tells that his "eyes ran over the page
and his heart perceived the sense."

Alone in my room at night, a row of votive candles
quivering, I practice the miraculous
learning of Ambrose. My tongue reclines
in the chatterbox of my mouth,
a calliope fitted with steam whistles and keys.

O blabbermouth. O magpie, imitator of words—
how you want to prattle. My index finger taps,
longing to guide my tired eyes
across the print.

But it is the rose window of my heart that struggles
to let in the light. Heart in your chancel,
locked in a lattice of ligament and rib,
may you see the wisdom that waits in the silent
word upon the page.

John Milton Stops By

Blake wrote only when the whirl of angels
told him to, and then the words flew about the room
in all directions. It is evening

two hundred years later. I light a beeswax candle
and drop to my knees, looking for a vision.

How fond animals must have been of Blake, his blunted
nose and massive head. "All wholesome food is caught
without trap or net," he wrote in *Hell's Proverbs*.

How is it that inspiration comes to us?
I picture the slit of a knife, the lifeblood flowing down.

Blood is such a simple grace: transparent plasma,
white blood cells, platelets and proteins,
hormones and salts. It carries the heavens,

the world with its catacombs and tombs, salvation
in a cup and contagion in a drop.

Milton stops by in his resurrected flesh to gossip
about fallen angels. He is still taken with Satan's soliloquy
—how he flies along the wall with weary wings

looking for a place to land, and the pile of alabaster rock
that climbs from earth to the clouds with only one entrance.

It is night three hundred fifty years later. A few words
dancing on the tongue, from the library
of old memories where most things can be told.

Physiognomy

Washes and razors for foofoos... for me freckles and a bristling beard.
                                                        —Walt Whitman

No wonder I did not find you at the barber shop
in Camden, lolling in the chair, mounds
of shaving cream heaped upon your ruddy face.
The whip of the straight razor on the strop, its scrape
and blather, is not your song, Celebrant of the Body.

You adore the tufts of hair on chin, cheeks and throat:
muttonchops, thatch of matted hair, the bristle
and stubble of five-o-clock shadow, goatees
and drooping mustaches, even the curl of hair spiraling
from ears and unfurling out of nostrils.

Lay your fingertips on your beard like a planchette
of prophecy and spell the names of the new priests.
Your freckles and moles are printer's marks, type
set by the hand of God. On your skin I smell the aroma
of ink, the fume of a new humanity.

Admit it now: drunk on bliss you woke one morning
in rivergrass, the Divine streaming from your pores,
dripping from your locks. And your beard
enchanted as well, woven with thistledown, river icicles,
cottonwood and wildvine.

From its tangled fleece butterflies rise, swallowtails
with yellow and blue markings. One settles on your finger,
opening and closing her wings like an iridescent book,
and you breathing the perfume of her dust, reading
the scripture of her body.

Bibliomancy

Walk down any row—past science and gardening,
or decimals and call numbers with their own code,
and pause before a shelf.

The titles on the spine do not matter,
whether buckram or vellum, the gold tooling,
slipcover, or dust jacket.

Even if you do not know the question
—an answer waits for you.
Think of the volumes as animate beings, bound

and then stacked one next to another, across centuries
and cultures, content to ponder their thoughts,
patiently biding their time.

They've grown used to the sexual high jinks
of the wingless book lice, their insatiable
hunger for vowels, and silverfish with a taste for starch.

Bibliomancy is not a passage from the holy book
chosen at random, for who is to say which book is holy,
and which is not?

Library and bookstore are temple, monastery,
cloistered abbey of the living and dead, devoted
to the virtuous life of books.

And there is no random, is there?—everything strung
together, chaos simply more information
unrolling the lines of blueprint and design.

Synchronicity links mind to matter: a long lost friend
remembered an instant before the phone rings,
a bridge that appears at eerie moments to walk us across.

An event strings lights onto a state of mind
to remind us chance is not blind, clicking along with a cane.
Reaching up and taking down one volume

you are dumbfounded to open and read from the book
that knows the story of your life—
in which the words that wake you are written.

Insomnia

The wide awake words are milling about,
twiddling their thumbs
and mumbling under their breath.
They are tired of being put to bed
and told to stop their yammering.
In the thick of night they knock on my door,
come in carrying their little black bags
packed with smelling salts and a game of go.
They want to travel to Mesopotamia
to search for the Tower of Babel,
climb its steps and say a prayer
for the world's many tongues.
The sleepless words think paradise is a realm
where all the eyelids have vanished.
At four in the morning they read Rumi
aloud and sniff for the perfume
of the Beloved under the stars
while twirling like dervishes.
They claim to have seen things: the world
quivering like a rabbit,
heart of the red rose beating,
a ladder that leads to heaven.
When the sun shuffles across the sky
wearing its pink robe, they begin to yawn.
And when the cuckoo hurries
through the wooden doors of the clock—
they pack up, counting the hours
as the hands fly around
spiraling toward the ecstasy
of night.

Curses for He Who Borrows & Returns
Not a Book
after the monastery library of San Pedro, Barcelona

May the kept book change to a serpent in his hands,
rise up and bite him squarely on the nose.
At that, let him begin to bray like a donkey in heat
and may all his members then shrivel.
From this great pain, may he grovel for mercy,
singing in falsetto as he slowly decomposes.
Let bookworms nibble at his entrails as a sign
of the *Worm that dieth not*.

He must have seen that worm at the heart of an apple,
eating its way past the pure binding of skin
to nest at the center near the seeds.
He has heard the *hssssss* from the infamous tree,
beheld the long exile out of the garden.
Indeed he has come to resemble a worm,
grown lean and segmented like an earthworm
or the leech used to bleed a patient, treat a bruise.

When he travels by boat across the final river,
straddling the bench above the dank water,
may he see all manner of friends beyond an impassable door
seated on sofas soft as clouds and reading in moonlight.
Let him find a stack of books with blank pages,
his reading glasses having lost their lenses,
and beneath a lampshade pleated like angel wings—
the fine wire of the filament burnt and snapped in two.

Bestiary

Already the knowing animals are aware that we are not really
at home in our interpreted world.
                    —Rainer Maria Rilke

Did he learn this on barefoot walks through wet fields
with Salomé? She taught him not to eat the meat

of animals, but the flesh of fruit and vegetable,
and the breads (risen, flat, dusted with flour or seeds).

Did she part the branches of trees and call the names:
nestling, or bird of prey? Did she push aside bushes
calling: creeping thing, poor beast of burden?

Was it then he saw how the animals merely tolerate us
now—having lost all hope, weary even of our stories?

Or was it when Rodin sent him out into the world
to *see*? For weeks he stood in the Paris zoo watching
the black beast in its cage.

At last he could feel the big cat's desolation, and took
within his heart the terrible truth.

He learned to leave even his name behind. He learned
how easily earth will go on, without the most wise
and petulant of her creatures.

Nothing Is What It Seems to Be

Even when reading, strange things take place.
Small gods turn up in the intricate details
of punctuation. The ampersand says "the sign by itself
is the word." The dots of ellipses gather together
in threes and fours, to talk of an exalted unseen presence.

I turn a page and the portly angels of Giotto float
into the room. They scrunch their pallid faces and sigh.
And great black bulls run down from the photograph
of a cave wall. They wind through corridors, stomping
with desire, horns arcing at last into light.

Once more I see Joanie Love in the shiny hoop of her bed.
Gold water flows up the tube and into her body.
Bed sores shrink back to bone, the skin on her thighs
now smooth as flannelette. She waves from the backseat
of a car by the side of a dark road. The truck bearing down
on her makes a sudden turn.

The archives of our lives open up. Images and documents
flutter and rise, the yellowing papers of birth and death
turn white as wood pulp, reenter the trees.
We watch flat entities come to life and take flight.
Left standing at break of day, we are learning
to move about in time.

Goethe's Theory of Color

If color is the speech of nature's soul,
then nature speaks hyacinth, lavender

and larkspur, purple prose and heliotrope—
any plant that turns toward the sun.

When Newton looked into a prism,
he saw a beam of light as a flux of corpuscles.

Five thousand angstroms of a scientist's green
tell me nothing of your hazel eyes,

the retina with its cones and rods that secrete
their visual purple. And what of color's aura:

mother of pearl on a soap bubble, trail
of a garden snail, the sheen of heated metal.

The feathers of a gray pigeon shimmer green
and violet in the day's dazzlement of light.

Nature speaks these white breasts, the sunburned
brown of your forearm,

the thin blue vein in your thigh that pulses
as you pull me down toward you.

Wounded Child

She wants to be heard, waits patient as earth,
tilling her garden of memories.

Her plants grow tall: thyme, forget me not,
passion flower, purple chokeweed.

She catches tears in hollowed hands,
lets the salt leach out. Soon there is water

for dousing, each plant giving itself to form,
each seed grasping its singular destiny.

You might think hers is a solitary life,
yet she has an abundance of company.

Child after child wait in beds of creeper
and vinegrub, in gardens of tangle and rue.

They stand, bare faces to the sun, stunned,
never aging. They stay eight, nine, thirteen

forever, knobby knees and toothy smiles,
there—among the stalks and leaves, sighing.

Blue Flower, Red Moon

We are the children who never grow up
defilement sewn
into our bodies and bones.

We look young as the day those hands
first entered us
opening the seams of soft flesh.

Our faces are bewildered, pale as moons,
eyes set wide apart and tucked open.
We have learned to smile, swollen lips

folded under, pink tip of the tongue stilled,
white teeth set like little
markers in our violated mouths.

In our hands scissors can mar the arms,
cold blades open and close
to leave their scars.

In no time at all we learn to make
our own pattern
called hem of sorrow, collar of shame.

At night we tie remnants into rags
that we store in pillow cases
or braid into rugs to silence the floor.

We learn the fine art of appliqué
cut pieces from new cloth
(gold star, blue flower, red moon)

to sew on the surface of the old.
We learn to stitch the word *forgiven*
onto our tattered bodies.

Wingspun

For Chrissy Clausen, 1952-1971

Mornings she descended the stairs and waited by the stove,
stirring oatmeal and apples in a pot. The old tree
in the backyard stretched its branches.

The land unfolded: acres of forest, the chapel
of white brick, graveyard beside the river, voices calling.

Evenings she braided her hair and folded paper into birds.
Japanese cranes and songbirds swung in the quiet air.

On her bedroom walls hung drawings of the island
in St. Mary's River. In winter she walked on its shroud,
pretending she lived in silence on an ice floe.

She looked near tree stumps for nature spirits, believed
they lived in wild places—in thickets or a tangle of brush.
Instead she found a desolate field of fire.

None of us could foresee how the blaze would leap
to gather her in its billowing, how her body would burn.

Five days she hesitated between this world and the next.
The old tree grew a new ring, and paper birds

flew from the branches. She was always an angel,
even then, living higher in the pale house,
lingering among the trees.

Poet as Oracle

She speaks in the voice of flowers, forgotten gods,
the proverbial seasons. She loves the bronze coins
with square holes at their center—

how when flung six times they tell of good fortune:
when to set out in a small boat on the great sea.
She echoes the turnings of things.

On the stage of a mystery play she sees a man
and woman tumble from a stone tower.
Dressed as the fool in blue, she sets out.

Behind her tiptoe a Greek priest and the grim
reaper in his rumpled black cloak. A maiden follows,
tipping water from a pitcher.

She dreams of joining the round of heavenly bodies,
the slow dance of stars and planets, sun
and moon on its way to the seventh house.

She dives into the darkness, face streaked crimson
with the blood of berries. Hunting for visions
she returns, bearing tokens and holy bones.

Clan of a desert tribe, she wears the mask of insect
and tree, rides in the belly of a fox, drops like scat
to read the language of paw prints.

On woodbark and paper pressed from trees
she marks the calligraphy of her visions, makes
worlds to fit in the palm of her hand.

The Moon

Your sweet face hangs bruised in the night sky.
You breathe deeply and tides rise. The holy week
of women draws near.

One summer I slept outside on soft new grass
and learned to touch myself from a moon eyed boy.
You stared down from the sea of tranquility.

I could run these fingers over your face, stroke
the pockmarked mounds, smooth land fine as silt.
My fingertips would tap out the secrets of you.

Your craters and seas talk to us across space.
If we think of you as dead, it must be our own
emptiness we tell of.

Behind the face that swells then dwindles to a lopsided
grin, a dark side we do not see, and beyond—
the smoldering light of stars.

What Are You Doing Here, García Lorca?

In Andalusia, along the blue Mediterranean Sea,
grapevines stretch their thin gray arms
to you. The sour oranges of Seville sing your name.
Inside the reddish rind, seeds weep with joy.
I want to let everyone know you are still alive.

You said that a thread travels through the hearts
of all poor children, pulled taut through purse strings.
But who among us is not poor,
having forgotten how to see the black angels
unfolding their handkerchiefs?

Tell me, where do you go in those moments of trance?
A flamenco guitar carved from cypress, your right hand
rattling the strings. Here comes that deep song.
Play for us, you who were murdered for loving men.
I adore your flat footed waddle.

Come along now. Bring the mask of death,
hounds from their graveyard. That uncanny way of yours,
reading the clues the world lays before you. You tell
the story of your life before it is lived, talk always
of *la muerte*, flirt with death in its dark robes.

So, you are never to sleep: in the ground, in the green
binding of books, in yellow teeth chattering
in moonlight. Tomorrow another sun will rise,
spreading its bright red skirts like a new wound
upon the sallow sea.

Four: Illusions of the Body

On Fire

Those who die the death of fire...they live forever.
—Thomas Merton

It begins as combustion, this making
of heat and light,
the turning of body into blaze.

She is last seen in a field, on fire.
Flames tongue her cuffs, unbutton her collar,
lick both sleeves.

She runs clothed in red firelight.
Her hair vanishes into ash, her body drops
like a charred doll.

A monk on the other side of the world
falls beneath a spinning fan. What force
pulls this whirl of wind and fire downward?

Smoke rises, leaving behind a holy relic.
He foresaw this as a blessed passing:
death by fire in the sign of Aries.

One instant, the illusion of a solid body;
the next, candle ends and kindling.
The remnants of a life rise up.

Sunlight descending into trees.

Strategies of the Feminine

Running hunched to the ground darkbodied by the shrubs,
we think first it is a cat, but then the long scaly tail
gives it away. The opossum scurries into an opening
between the pyracantha.

Opossums will eat almost anything: grasshoppers,
caterpillars, carrion, acorns, wild cherries, persimmons.
The soft ruddy body of the persimmon, like a ripe
breast in a warm hand.

Chinese artists adored the orangey red fruit.
In the Sung dynasty, Mu-ch'i painted *Six Persimmons*—
goddess of compassion at the center, scroll of monkeys
and a marshbird on either side.

Years ago, I woke in a cabin on the far coast.
Outside, an opossum dangled upside down in a tree.
For the shaman full of opossum spirit—things are dramatic,
blown out of proportion, the normal likely to be upended.

On backcountry roads when I see one lying motionless
along black pavement, I wonder if its pouch holds a litter—
born blind, naked and grublike, having crawled
from the womb, hungry for milk, and weakening?

Or is it merely playing dead, lying on its side, corners
of the mouth drawn back and drooling?
The beady black eyes stare straight ahead, still as glass.
Opossum shamans take such posturing to heart.

These shamans love all forms of diversion and distraction:
the opposable toe tucked to each hind foot,
a tree hidden in an acorn, the tang of the cherry,
its hard pit—a tactic within the wild purple fruit.

Pomegranate

Under the scrawny winter branches,
down among the bending roots, we buried
the small animal. He was not yet cold.

His soft tawny fur still shone, his eyes stared
forward: luminous and black.

Into the box lined with tissue paper we tucked
a lettuce leaf, oats and seeds for his journey.
I wanted to lay my hand on your shoulder.

You said a prayer, forgave the predatory cat,
and promised to eat the first fruit.

In May the pomegranate bush turned
miraculously green once again, sprouting orange
flowers and the leathery fruit.

The red flesh the prophet Muhammad said
purges us of envy and hate.

Splitting one open, you push your thumbs
through its chambers, fingers bent to scoop
the cool tart seeds.

We eat mouthful after mouthful, staining our lips
and tongues blood red.

Already skin and teeth and tiny bones
are giving themselves up to the dark earth.
Already your fierce ache has lessened.

Cathedral

Down the cobbled walkway that leads to the sea,
past the spiny cactus plants,
gray stones are laid in baked clay. Terra cotta.

This burnt earth. We are a procession
wobbling on its way, bones tilted at odd angles,
the whole line a little skewed.

Workmen stand off to one side leaning
on their shovels, dark eyes taking in our footsteps.
We pass a mound of relics:
ropes of kelp, broken lipped shells, one sandal.

The ocean works a ritual, lures our heartbeat
to its rhythm, ushers the soul out of exile
back into the body. It is a simple act of element
and phase, breath and wave.

Overhead three white pelicans fly by.
From the mouth of one dangles a wiggling fish.
A slight tip of the heavy bill and the fish
slips down into the immense pouch.

The workers see this. We each witness
a transfiguration: water to air, fish into flight,
and above it all the cerulean blue vault of the sky.

Hellhole Canyon

I believe that I am in hell, therefore I am there.
                    —Arthur Rimbaud

Settlers named it Hell Creek for the crossing,
the slippery descent down a ravine,
ticks that wait in the brush for the scent of man.

Rattlesnakes shake their dry beads. The buzzing
empties the mind, parches the lips,
causes the heart to knock in its rickety crate.

Monkey flowers bloom. Poke the stamen
with a stick and the flower shuts tight.
Seedpods of wild cucumber, spikey green

and the size of a fist, dangle from manzanita.
The roots of the mandrake curl like an embryo
or a person crouching in fear.

The trail is spotted by sunlight and gleaming leaves.
Hell has never looked so good.
Wade across. Enter the glade where rock walls

darken with moss. The air turns clammy
and a sound comes like the pluck of wings.
It is a place not far from here.

The Doorway

I was young and almost ridiculous that year, riding the train
from Mexicali to Mexico City, three days and nights
stiff as a statue on the wooden seats.

A woman held a red rooster in a cage on her lap.
Someone carried a pig aboard and it squealed for hours.
The air smelled of feathers and dung.

Sweat ran down my face, thick as blood.
At last I stood before the door, taken from an Aztec
prison, of the pink hacienda beyond Cuernavaca.

I rang a wrought iron bell and a man opened the door.
A gold amulet dangled from a chain around his neck,
nested in the silver hairs of his chest.

He led me past the pool, down worn steps and corridors,
into a wine cellar where the bottles wore his name.
We walked over terra cotta tiles, heard Aztecan

voices, saw a young girl crying out, black hair flung
like wings. Rubbed with red powder, she was dressed
in bark cloth and tied with woven rope.

Her heart thrashed about in the sacristy of her chest.
I left the man to his chambers and his artifacts,
did not linger in that house of voices.

Late at night I tell the girl a story, how she flees
from the priests and their rituals. She cuts loose the ropes.
Rain falls like tears and the corn grows tall as trees.

Wheel of Becoming

For a long time you have been wandering.
Once you passed through a place where life itself
was tedious: anything you wanted was yours,
simply by thinking of it.

You awoke to travel the jungles of Peru,
paddled up the Napo River to Iquitos.
Slipping past birdsong and the snakes with languid
tongues, you knew their twitter and hiss.

A lifetime later near Tecate, you passed by agave
and prickly pear, whispering *El Norte*.
Sand turned your tongue thick. You leaned out
over a canyon far above the arroyo
but in the end you were too frightened to fly.

Even so, the return to spiritbody feels good.
You remember some of the many lives you lived,
where you were born, sometimes for what reason.
In the distance you hear a sibilant sound,
a whooshing of rush and flow.

Drawn to a man and woman, you hover above
their bed. The tired springs creak and sigh.
You fall toward their bodies, jostle tight into a tender
tube. The light all around glows pink and red.
You are strung to a trellis of fibers and tubules.

There was a thought you meant to hold
near as a heartbeat. Soon you will sway
within the belly of a shallow blue sea, curled up
like a question mark.

Seven Ways of Divination

1) Sychomancy—divination with leaves of the fig tree

I am particularly fond of figs,
the multitude of female flowers
inside a fleshy vesicle,
the tiny seeds and soft purple flesh,
how they resemble the scrotum.
The fig leaf is loincloth,
dhoti, foliage on a statue's
male genitalia. A leaf is not found
on the archaic torso of Apollo,
armless yet lovely,
where the amiable head
of the penis lies on its plush bed.
But in paintings of Adam
after the fall, there it is—
plucked from the garden.
Pull a leaf from a fig tree
and write a question on it.
Place the leaf in the sun to dry.
Does her belly swell with desire?
Will he be faithful for fourteen years?
A leaf that begins to shrivel,
that starts to parch
and wither, is saying: no.
The leaf that lingers,
cells bustling under the green
epithelium, is saying: yes.

2) *Alphitomancy—divination by barley in an oracular trial*

To learn if a lover is unfaithful,
bake a loaf of barley bread.
Mix one cup warm well water,
a sprinkle of yeast, a pinch of salt,
three cups barley flour ground by stone,
two spoonfuls of oil.
Knead till it glistens,
pulling its body together.
Shape into a loaf and let rise.
Bake till a broomstraw stuck
in the center comes out clean.
Bring your lover a slice
and have him say:
"If I am deceiving you—
may this bread come foul upon me."
Because he does not believe
in barley, he will heedlessly agree.
When he begins to writhe
on the floor, flatulence may appear
like an apocalyptic wind
that blows the answer in.

3) *Oomancy—divination by eggs*

For this ancient art taught by Orpheus,
I favor a newly laid egg.
Hold it above a bowl of hot water,
take a hatpin and poke it in the small end.
This might bring back memories
of Eastertide, blowing
an egg empty: cheeks puffed up,

eyes straining, the veins
in the neck wriggling like worms
as you make what was once
a pagan amulet of fertility.
Into the bowl drip a goodly amount
of eggwhite. Repeat again
and again the question
in search of an answer.
Patterns will appear, albumen drifting
in its watery limelight. A pouch
of plump coins. A torn heart.
A homunculus, limp arms
floating, slack mouth about to speak.

4) *Tyromancy—divination by holes and mold in cheese*

The fungi and holes in cheese
read like tea leaves.
Mold spores of bleu cheese
(pressed curd of goat milk)
tunnel into the lump of matter.
Pose a question and look
on the first symbol seen.
The two lobed hole like a heart
hints at love. A diamond shape
with its four equal sides
is a message to strive for perfection.
A cabbage shape of moldy leaves
(gray network of nappy filaments)
tells of jealousy, envy
from a false friend.
A frog with his forked tongue
tells of trouble for someone
who jumps to conclusions.

5) *Felidomancy—divination by cats*

It is not true cats have nine lives.
When my cat Sambo died
I mourned three days,
shaved off my eyebrows
just as the Egyptians did.
Ignore the stories that early Christians
tortured cats, burned them
at the stake alongside witches.
Cats are not deities or devils.
Wise catcher of rats and mice,
maker of mew and purr,
a cat will let you stroke her
if she wishes. Ask a question
and if she sneezes it will rain.
If she walks across your path
it is bad fortune
(unless you live in Britain
where it is auspicious).
When Sambo stared through slitted eyes
and licked his long curved claws,
the answer was always no.

6) *Nephelomancy—the prophecy of clouds*

Particles of water
and ice clustered in air:
fleecy cirrus clouds high up
and white, layers of stratus
much lower down,
dome shaped cumulus,
their permutations
point out the shape of things to come.

Lie down on the ground.
Look up through blue sky.
There is a cloud shaped like a patient
asleep on a table. It means an old man
in a dry year (a bowl of rotted peaches
in the fridge) who will wake
and find love at last.
I have seen clouds like archangels,
their wings widening
as they pass by, a cloud bulging
like a mushroom, gray evanescence
looking outward at us.

7) *Hepatomancy—liver gazing*

There is a long history of it: foretelling
the future by studying the liver
of sacrificial animals.
The prophet Ezekiel says:
"For the king of Babylon
stood at the parting of the way,
at the head of the two ways,
to use divination:
he made his arrows bright,
he consulted with images,
he looked in the liver."
Clay and bronze models
come from the Middle East,
Etruscans and Hittites, the Sumerians
down on their knees
looking for six thousand
variations in shape and size.
On the floor before them, a pyramid

of fleshy tissue rises
from the base of the gall bladder.
If large and firm, it is a good omen.
When stunted or misshapen,
it foretells disaster.
The sacrificial signs
are making their way through
the small lobes of the liver,
the vessels and cells, the five ligaments.
I can almost divine a revelation
waiting to unfold,
some hidden wisdom.

Herself Divined

You come from some walled town, you bring its sorcery with you.
—H.D.

Born to a family of scientists,
she grew up peering through eyepieces:
gazing into the heavens with their vast tracks
of stars, looking down into drops of pondwater
heavy with diatoms and algae.

A bearded tutor lured her to Greece. For years
she feasted on slain deer, brown olives
fat and soaked in oil, the white cheese from goats.
She was a Greek maidengod, lean and willowy,
with knotted hair and wide eyes.

She woke to a pagan vision: star lore, table
tipping, the secret knowing of numbers.
A Moravian ancestor stood maternal at her shoulder,
teaching her the direct lineage and its illumination—
from maker to made.

She believed the stroke of a poet's pen
can realign the world. The modern god of chaos
welcomed once more bows down, meek before her.
Still we hear her spirit rapping, her whispering,
poetry is the highest science.

Homoerotica

She dreams of a house filled with light
and window boxes of lobelia and sweet william,
content in their holders, roots unlikely to outgrow
the wooden boxes on the sill.

Morning crawls from under a quilt of colors
as the breeze licks hips and thighs.
Two women turn toward one another, tumble
into familiar arms, touch the swollen places,
follow the deep pattern of stroke and sigh.

She rises, and in the kitchen cuts oranges
for the orioles who nest beyond the door.
Pushing the sticky halves onto a honeysuckle bush,
she listens for the clear sweet call.

Tomorrow she will plant white impatiens
along the stone walkway, the ripe pods bursting open
when touched. She prefers perennials, except
for this one indulgence: in the shady area out front,
a trail of pure white among the shadows.

In Sunday worship she reflects on these acts,
yearns to share the scent of earth on her fingers,
the lovely musky smell of women and soil,
the sanctity of each delving.

Killing the Ants

Flies are shooed from my house, spiders coaxed
into a glass and carried to the flower bed
to spin among the azaleas. But ants with their narrow
stalks and biting mouthparts will not leave.

Mornings they line up along the countertop,
moving out of the toaster with its scullery of crumbs.
They like kibbles of pet food and tupelo honey
left to clot in a spoon.

Along the baseboards, I lay down lines of Chinese chalk,
borax and coffee grounds, and still they persist.
At night I dream of the lesser anteater with its long sticky
tongue and love of soft bellied bugs.

I have not seen ants making love or burying their dead,
but I know something of the way they live:
soldiers defending their colonies,
tailor ants sewing plush nests from the silk of offspring,
the honey ant swollen like a golden raisin.

If hell is the place we go, bodiless yet weighted down
by guilt, how long will it take until I am forgiven
for waging my contemptible war on them?
I envision the trial over ant bodies
that by the time of my death number tens of thousands.

In the courtroom of my mind, the ants are spoken for
by two sets of jaws that gesticulate madly,
an immense head, antennae long as my forearm.
The diminutive waist captivates me. The scent of formic
acid drifts like an acrid perfume.

Telling the Bees

When the old man draws his last breath,
the child must visit the hives. She walks down the path
of yellow pasture grass, rattling a chain of keys.

Pear trees dip their branches into tall grass.
Bees crawl on fallen fruit with their thick hind feet,
or take to the air wearing their bulky coats
made from feathery hairs.

The hives stand like a cluster of wooden churches.
She taps on the white walls to tell the bees he is gone.
Later, women will tie black crepe to the hives
and bring plates of sweets for the bees.

She thinks what a good man he was, kind and unruffled.
Whenever he was stung, he scraped the stinger out
with a thin blade. He said bees despise bad language
and so he was mindful never to curse.

She loves the bees' gift for music, their operatic
buzzing and dancing, the slowbellied tumble
toward nectar, and what he told her, how bees are shells
for the souls of the dead.

She spends long hours lying in the field,
staring up through green leaves filled with leafblood,
wondering which humming body might be his.

The Stout Bodied Fly

Despised fly with your piercing mouthpiece
and one pair of usable wings
—the second pair but little knobs to balance by,
like gyroscopes in flight—
a humble, lowly species.

Fishing lures imitate you with feathers,
tinsel, and colored thread. When cast overhead,
the line singing, they land on a quiet pond to wait
for the gulping mouth of trout.

How your legless larvae love the foul things.
They writhe in heaps of dung and muck,
revel in the rot of matter.
In the compost pile, the burst tomatoes are alive
with the seethe and stir of maggots.

Issa loved you among the world's small creatures,
how you twist your hands and feet,
and in the temple, mimic the pious people
fingering their prayer beads.

The hairs on your feet stick to slippery surfaces
and so you walk like a small miracle
up the side of a wall, veined wings folded,
windows of a tiny, dark church.

How does the world look through your compound
eyes, the facets like four thousand lenses?
Some day you will trail your blue green
belly over my closed eyelids, the last thing
I hear—buzzing.

Last Rites

When I am dead, let my body rest for three days.
Do not gather around me, weeping,
gnashing your teeth and sighing, to pull my soul back
into its forsaken bag of bones.

Read to me from the Book of the Dead.
Tell me not to fear the demons, the green woman
with a bird's face, or the hungry ghosts on the yellow path.
Remind me they are merely the play of my own mind.

On the fourth day, when I am placed upon the movable
tray before the doors to the great fire,
take off my ring, the gold band with one diamond
and the pink and green leaves. Wear it.

When you are handed the carton of dust and bone,
do not buy a porcelain urn. Instead sprinkle me high up
in the Cuyamaca mountains, under the spindly
branches of a scrub oak.

Look for me when you too cross over. I will be waiting
just beyond the luminous tunnel, wearing bluejeans,
my purple shirt, heavy shoes—frantic to tell you
about the next implausible realm.

Notes

Buddha telling of those: In the *Anguttara Nikaya* the Buddha defines the practitioner of magic: "Without sinking he walks on water as if on earth.... With his hand he touches and strokes the sun and the moon."

Blake wrote only when the whirl of angels told him to: Peter Ackroyd relates this in his biography of William Blake.

A monk on the other side of the world: Thomas Merton had prophesied such a death for himself. In a letter he wrote, "Those who die the death of fire—the death which Christianity was to call martyrdom, and which Herakleitos definitely believed was a witness to the Fire and the Logos ... they live forever."

Remind me not to fear the demons: Chögyam Trungpa comments on *The Tibetan Book of the Dead* that visions of wrathful and peaceful deities happen continually during living and dying, indeed, at this very moment.

The Richard Snyder Publication Series

This book is the fourth in a series honoring the memory of Richard Snyder (1925-1986), poet, fiction writer, playwright and longtime professor of English at Ashland University. Snyder served for fifteen years as English Department chair, and was co-founder (in 1969) and co-editor of The Ashland Poetry Press, an adjunct of the university. He was also co-founder of the Creative Writing major at the school, one of the first on the undergraduate level in the country. In selecting the manuscript for this book, the editors kept in mind Snyder's tenacious dedication to craftsmanship and thematic integrity.

Snyder Award Winners:

1997: Wendy Battin for *Little Apocalypse*
1998: David Ray for *Demons in the Diner*
1999: Philip Brady for *Weal*
2000: Jan Lee Ande for *Instructions for Walking on Water*